IN ANCIENT EGYPT

THE
PHARAOHS

CONTENTS

SALIMA IKRAM

Illustrations by Salah Hassab

HOOPOE BOOKS

WHO WERE THE PHARAOHS?

T he rulers of ancient Egypt are called pharaohs. The word
pharaoh comes from the ancient Egyptian words "pr aa",
meaning "the Great House". This was the title used for the
king because he lived in a palace, the largest house in all of
Egypt.

The pharaoh was the most powerful person in all of Egypt. The
Egyptians believed that the pharaoh was a god on earth and had
absolute power over everything. He was thought to be the hawk-
god Horus. He was the king, a god, the high priest for all the
gods, the head of the army and the owner of all the riches of
Egypt. He was responsible for the people of Egypt and had to
make sure they did not suffer from injustice, starvation or want.

An ancient text advises the king:

"Don't be evil, kindness is good.
Make your memorial last through love of you,
Respect your nobles and care for your people.
Strengthen your borders, your frontier patrols.
Speak truth in your house
So that the officials of your kingdom respect you.
Do justice, then you endure on earth.
Calm the weeper, do not oppress people.
Beware of punishing unjustly,
Thus will the land be well-ordered!"

Right: The pharaoh Seti I wearing the blue
war crown and offering incense to a god

Alhough a pharaoh was expected to be good and just, this was not always the case. Some kings were bad and greedy, or just weak, and did not carry out their responsibilities. Sometimes these pharaohs were overthrown but at other times the people suffered until the pharaoh died and the next pharaoh succeeded to the throne.

Below: The Narmer Palette. At the top the pharaoh Narmer is wearing the Red Crown and inspecting his dead enemies. Their heads have been cut off and are lying between their feet. Why do you think the pharaoh is shown as much bigger than the others?

Above: The crook and flail

In Egyptian art the pharaoh can be recognised by several things. In paintings he is the largest person shown, apart from the gods. They are the same size as pharaoh because he was also a god. He wears a crown and carries a crook and flail. The crook is what shepherds use to care for sheep and means that the king looks after his people. The flail is a kind of whip and means that the king is a judge who gives justice and punishes wrong-doers or invaders of his country.

The king often wears a beard which is not real but made of gold and semi-precious stones. The beard is attached to his face with hooks over the ears. We do not really know what the beard meant; possibly that the king is a god, because gods are the only others who wear false beards. The king also had a bull's tail attached behind him, because bulls were considered powerful animals. One of the titles of the king is "Mighty Bull". Another animal associated with the king was the lion, the king of beasts.

Below: These two pharaohs wear tails, elaborate head-dresses and false beards. Each one holds a key of life because pharaohs were supposed to live for a long time

The Nile river, the main source of water in Egypt, flows from south to north. The south was therefore called Upper Egypt and the north Lower Egypt. Upper Egypt consists of thin strips of land beside the river that are good for growing crops. Lower Egypt is a large triangle of land with many small branches of the Nile. Lower Egypt is also called the Delta because the Greek letter "delta" (Δ) looks like a triangle upside down.

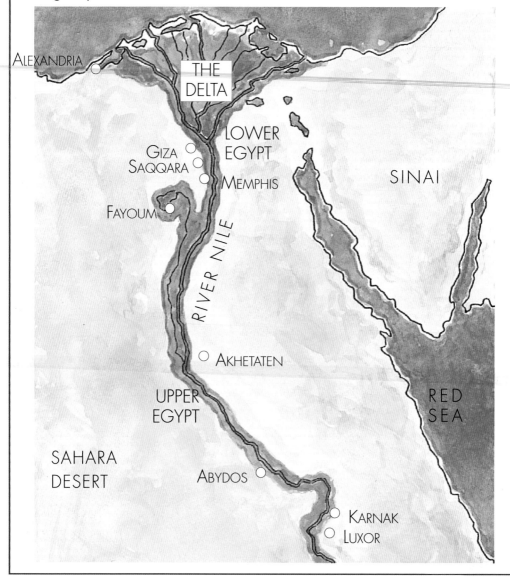

Other clothes and symbols of the pharaoh came from the Egyptians' ideas about their country. Because of the idea of Egypt being divided into Upper and Lower parts it was sometimes called "the Two Lands". One of the king of Egypt's titles was Lord of the Two Lands. The ancient Egyptians had symbols for the two parts of their country: a lotus flower for Upper Egypt and a papyrus plant for Lower Egypt. Often pictures on thrones show the lotus and papyrus tied together to represent the unification of the two parts of Egypt.

Above: In the centre of this stone the lotus (with three petals) and papyrus are tied together to show the unification of Upper and Lower Egypt. The two holes are where the broken stone was repaired in ancient times

Each part of the country was also represented by a goddess in the shape of an animal. Wadjet, the cobra-goddess, stood for Lower Egypt, and Nekhbet, the vulture-goddess, stood for Upper Egypt. Sometimes the heads of both these animals were made of gold and used as decoration on the front of the "nemes" head-dress (a type of crown) of the pharaoh.

Left: Nekhbet and Wadjet sitting on baskets

The papyrus plant was grown mainly in the Delta, which made it an obvious symbol for Lower Egypt. It was used to make the earliest form of paper, and is the origin of the English word paper. The stalks were used for boat-building and one can even eat parts of the plant.

The king also had separate crowns for each part of the country: the Red Crown for Lower Egypt and the White Crown for Upper Egypt. When he wanted to show that he was the head of a united Egypt he wore the double crown, which was a combination of the red and white crowns. Unfortunately, although we have pictures and statues showing the king wearing these two crowns we have never found any real crowns, so we do not know what they were made of nor how they were made.

What do *you* think the crowns were made of?

From left to right: The Double Crown, the White Crown, the Nemes head-dress, and the Red Crown

The king had different names for different occasions. Some of these names are easy to find because they were written inside a cartouche. The cartouche is an oval with a stick on one side, which separates the king's name from the rest of the hieroglyphs.

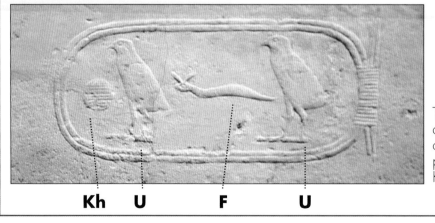

The cartouche of the pharaoh Khufu

Kh　　**U**　　**F**　　**U**

In order to show the people that he was strong and able to rule, the pharaoh had to perform an unusual ceremony. Every 30 years he had to put on his formal clothes, with the double crown, carry the crook and flail, and then run round a special court. This was called the Heb-Sed race. The court was larger than a modern football field. According to some texts the pharaoh had to run round the courtyard four times. If he did not fall down he was allowed to continue to rule. If he collapsed, a new pharaoh was chosen. Sometimes the pharaoh ran the Heb-Sed race after less than 30 years to prove he was still a strong ruler. There is no record of any pharaoh that fell over!

The Division of History

Egypt has one of the oldest civilisations in the world, starting more than 8,000 years ago. The way we learn about Egyptian history is by archaeological excavations and by reading histories written by the Greeks and Romans who lived in Egypt later on. We have no proper history books written by the ancient Egyptians themselves. We have found parts of King Lists, which are lists of the kings of ancient Egypt (for example on the wall of the temple of Seti I at Abydos), as well as some stories about certain kings from tombs and temple walls. These lists tell us which kings followed which.

The way we divide Egyptian history comes from the divisions that Manetho, a priest in Egypt, made in a book which he wrote in about 270 BC. No complete example of Manetho's book has ever been found but other writers knew that his book was important and copied it. From their copies we can find out some of what Manetho said. Unfortunately books are easily damaged and these copies are not complete, so we still do not know the names of all the pharaohs or what they did.

Sometimes archaeologists find objects with the names of new pharaohs that are not on other lists; we can then fill some gaps in what we know of ancient Egyptian history. For example, the statue of a man in the Egyptian Museum in Cairo has the names of some early pharaohs on the shoulder.

Right: This king list from a temple at Abydos is the most important list still in place in Egypt. King Seti I ordered this to be carved to show that he was the rightful successor of the earlier pharaohs

Manetho divided Egypt's history into dynasties or groups of rulers who were often, but not always, related to each other. Manetho listed 30 dynasties, grouped together into long periods of time which Egyptologists call Kingdoms. There are three Kingdoms: the Old, the Middle and the New.

Sometimes there was fighting between the Pharaoh and his nobles, or invasions from outside, and several different people ruled different parts of Egypt. These times came between the three kingdoms and are called the Intermediate Periods.

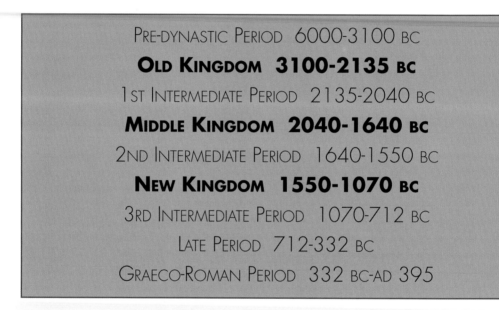

PRE-DYNASTIC PERIOD 6000-3100 BC

OLD KINGDOM 3100-2135 BC

1ST INTERMEDIATE PERIOD 2135-2040 BC

MIDDLE KINGDOM 2040-1640 BC

2ND INTERMEDIATE PERIOD 1640-1550 BC

NEW KINGDOM 1550-1070 BC

3RD INTERMEDIATE PERIOD 1070-712 BC

LATE PERIOD 712-332 BC

GRAECO-ROMAN PERIOD 332 BC-AD 395

At the end of pharaonic history there are two periods, the Late Period and the Graeco-Roman Period. At these times foreign rulers from Nubia, Persia, Greece and Rome ruled Egypt.

Right: A battle being fought during the 1st Intermediate Period, with soldiers being thrown from the battlements

THE OLD KINGDOM

In its earliest history, before Egypt was unified under one pharaoh, the country was made up of many small kingdoms with different kings. It was in the Pre-Dynastic Period that the Egyptians started farming, herding animals, building houses, making pottery and stone objects, and writing. However, no names of rulers are known from the Pre-Dynastic Period.

In 3100 BC a southern Egyptian king called Menes (Narmer was another of his names) battled with the rulers in the north and won. He became the first king of a unified Egypt, established the capital at Memphis, and started Egyptian Dynastic history.

It was during the Old Kingdom, which began with Menes, that all the basic characteristics of Egyptian civilization - such as its arts, architecture and customs - were established. At this time Egypt was very strong and had little contact with most of its neighbours.

There were six dynasties in the Old Kingdom, with many kings in each. Not much is known about most of these pharaohs although they built some of the biggest stone monuments in the world: the pyramids.

Left: The pyramids at Giza, near Cairo, where some of the pharaohs of the 4th Dynasty were buried

Above: The pharaoh Narmer (or Menes), wearing the White Crown and hitting his northern enemies with a mace. (This is the other side of the carving on page 4.) Below his feet lie the bodies of his enemies. What symbols of the pharaoh is he wearing?

15

Most of the pyramids in Egypt were built by the pharaohs of the Old and Middle Kingdoms as their tombs. The first pyramid in history was the Step Pyramid at Saqqara, built for King Djoser. The next important pyramid to be built was the Bent Pyramid of King Snefru. It was built at an angle because the Egyptians were still learning how to make pyramids with straight sides; they had to change the angle of this pyramid while they were building it, so that it did not fall down.

However, the three most famous pyramids were built at Giza. They include the biggest pyramid in the world, belonging to King Khufu (sometimes called Cheops). The pyramids at Giza all have straight sides and are called true pyramids.

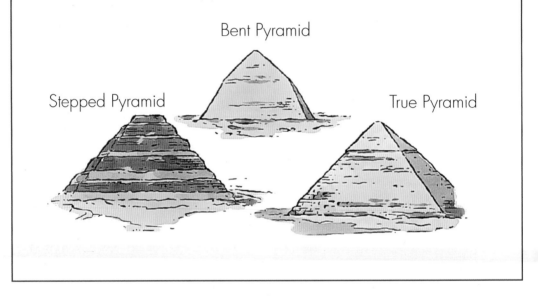

Bent Pyramid

Stepped Pyramid

True Pyramid

The Sixth Dynasty was the last in the Old Kingdom. During this time the pharaoh's power decreased and his nobles became more and more powerful. The last pharaoh in the dynasty was Pepi II who became pharaoh when he was six and died when he was about 100. Because Pepi ruled for more than 90 years and did many things during his reign which he and his nobles wrote about, we know more about him than we do about any other king of the Old Kingdom.

As soon as Pepi II came to the throne he ordered a trading mission to go to Nubia in the south of Egypt. The leader of the mission, a man called Harkhuf, found a Nubian pygmy there whom he planned to bring back as a companion for the young king. He wrote to Pepi II, telling him about the pygmy. The excited king sent a long letter to Harkhuf thanking him. Harkhuf was so proud to receive this letter that he had it carved on his tomb wall, which is how we know the story. King Pepi wrote:

"Come north to the palace at once! Hurry and bring with you this pygmy live, strong and healthy, to delight the heart of King Pepi who lives forever! When he goes down with you into the ship get good men to encircle him on deck so he does not fall into the water. When he lies down at night have people guard him so that no harm befalls him. I desire to see this pygmy more than anything else you bring!"

The 1st Intermediate Period

Unfortunately Pepi II ruled for so long and grew so old that his nobles took advantage of him and took away more and more of his power. When Pepi died, with no strong successor, the nobles started fighting among themselves and set up independent states all over Egypt. Several different dynasties ruled over parts of Egypt during this time, some for a very short time.

نموذج فصيلة من المشاة
نحيب ملوك
الدولة الوسطى - أسيوط

Model of a regiment of infantry

Some of what we know about this confusing time comes from the walls of tombs. The ancient Egyptians decorated their tombs and filled them with objects or models of objects and people that had been a part of their life. They believed that by doing this the objects would also be present in the afterlife. By studying the pictures on tomb walls, the objects that are found, and any texts that were written, archaeologists and historians can piece together what happened.

Tombs of this intermediate period show people wrestling and fighting, something that does not appear on tomb walls before this time. Models of soldiers carrying shields, spears, bows and arrows were also found in other tombs of this time.

An ancient Egyptian wrote of this period:

> *"The bowman is ready,*
> *The wrong-doer is everywhere,*
> *Men plunder the traveller."*

1ST INTERMEDIATE PERIOD
2135-2040 BC
The 9th, 10th and part of the 11th Dynasties made up this period.

Left: A model army of soldiers found in a tomb in Assiut, in Upper Egypt and now in the Egyptian Museum, Cairo. Soldiers in ancient Egypt had no armour and had to be quick with their shields to protect themselves.

19

THE MIDDLE KINGDOM

This kingdom started in the middle of the 11th Dynasty when Pharaoh Mentuhotep II from Upper Egypt fought several battles against other noblemen and became the ruler of all Egypt. On the west bank at Luxor an archaeologist found a tomb that contained the bodies of over 60 soldiers killed in one of these battles. The wounds on their bodies were still visible after nearly 4,000 years.

Some years later, when the country was again united and peaceful, Mentuhotep IV sent many expeditions throughout Egypt to obtain jewels and materials for his buildings. One of these expeditions was to the Wadi Hammamat granite quarries to get the stone for the pharaoh's sarcophagus (this is a stone box in which the coffin is placed).

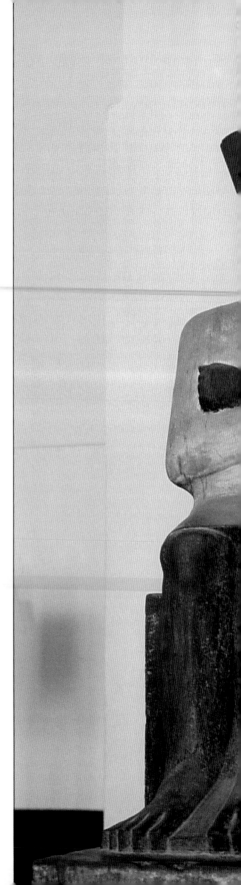

An inscription at Wadi Hammamat still survives. It reads:

> "His Majesty has sent the mayor with a troop of 10,000 men to bring a block of stone from the mountain."

There is a story that a gazelle came out of the desert and went to one particular stone. It lay down on the stone and had a baby! The workers chose that stone as a lid for the sarcophagus and took it back to the king.

THE MIDDLE KINGDOM
(2040-1640 BC)
This period consisted of half of the 11th Dynasty and all of the 12th, 13th and 14th dynasties.

Left: The pharaoh Mentuhotep II wearing the Red Crown. It is thought that he is painted black to represent the black soil of Egypt. The statue would have held the crook and flail in its hands. It was found near the king's tomb in Luxor.

THE 2ND INTERMEDIATE PERIOD

After the end of the 12th and 13th dynasties united Egypt again suffered problems as nobles started new dynasties and fought each other. Egypt was also invaded by people called the Hyksos who came from Western Asia and established a kingdom in Lower Egypt. Upper Egypt, however, was still ruled by a strong Egyptian dynasty. The Upper Egyptian king and the Hyksos king wanted to do battle but they needed an excuse. The Hyksos pharaoh Apophis wrote a letter to the Egyptian pharaoh Seqenenre Tao, saying:

> *"Let there be a withdrawal of your hippopotami from the canal because they do not let sleep come to me either in the day or night. Their noise is always in my ears!"*

It may seem incredible today but, because of this letter, Seqenenre Tao attacked the Hyksos and was killed in battle. His skull (now in the Egyptian Museum) shows wounds made by Hyksos axes. His successor, Kamose, continued the battle against the Hyksos, taking the fighting into Lower Egypt. He wrote:

> *"I travelled downstream to overthrow the Asiatics, my brave army in front of me like a breath of fire. I was upon Apophis as a hawk. I overthrew him, I razed his walls."*

Right: Seqenenre Tao's skull, showing the wounds he received

22

After Kamose's death the struggle against the Hyksos was continued by his brother Ahmose, who finally defeated the invaders completely and founded the 18th Dynasty.

Above: Hyksos warriors riding on their chariots towards the enemy

THE 2ND INTERMEDIATE PERIOD
This period included the 15th, 16th and 17th Dynasties.

Before the Hyksos came to Egypt there were only donkeys to ride. The Egyptians had no wheeled transport. The Hyksos brought chariots, horses, long-range bows and strong metal daggers into Egypt.

THE NEW KINGDOM

This was one of the richest periods in Egyptian history. Several strong pharaohs ruled a united country, traded with their neighbours, built temples, and even took over large parts of Syria, Palestine and Nubia.

Left: Hatshepsut dressed as a male pharaoh, offering jars of oil to the god Horus

The pharaoh Hatshepsut was the most famous female pharaoh in Egyptian history. She often dressed like a male pharaoh. She built a great temple at Deir el-Bahari near Luxor. The wall paintings show a trading expedition to the land of Punt (to the south of Egypt) from where incense trees, gold, ivory, ebony and animals were brought back. A carved stone at Karnak Temple (also near Luxor) says she also built "two obelisks each of hard granite, without seam, without joining together" in the temple. An obelisk is a very long rectangular pillar of stone, topped by a small pyramid which was covered in gold. The obelisk represented a sun-beam and was a symbol of the sun-god, Re.

Above: The very fat Queen of Punt followed by men carrying gifts for Hatshepsut

Left: Obelisk from Karnak Temple

The 18th, 19th and 20th Dynasties made up the New Kingdom. There were eleven pharaohs named Ramesses in the New Kingdom.

Hatshepsut's successor, Tutmoses III, was a great warrior who invaded Syria where he won the Battle of Megiddo. On a temple wall he wrote:

> *"His Majesty overwhelmed them at the head of his army and they fled headlong, abandoning their horses, their chariots of gold and silver."*

From Syria he brought back many strange plants and birds which were then carved onto the walls of the Festival Hall in Karnak Temple, a building he ordered to be constructed on his return.

25

Later on in the 18th Dynasty, the pharaoh Akhenaten changed the religion of ancient Egypt. He worshipped only one god - Aten, the sun - and banned all other Egyptian gods and their priests. A hymn to the Aten reads:

> *"Splendid you rise in heaven's lightland, O living Aten, creator of life! When you have dawned in the Eastern lightland you fill every land with beauty."*

Akhenaten also built a new capital city called Akhetaten, which means the Horizon of the Aten. The priests of the other gods were very unhappy because their gods were banned. Perhaps they had Akhenaten killed, although we do not know this for sure.

Akhenaten was succeeded by Tutankhamun who went back to the old religion with its many gods. Tutankhamun reigned for only nine years. However, he is the most famous pharaoh of all because his tomb in the Valley of the Kings is the only pharaoh's tomb to have been discovered complete. All his clothes, jewellery, tables, thrones, beds and chariots are now in the Egyptian Museum.

Ramesses II reigned for about 67 years, almost as long as Pepi II. He had over 100 children and built many temples throughout Egypt and Nubia. He fought several battles, the most famous of which was at Qadesh in Syria. At the Battle of Qadesh Ramesses II was tricked into being separated from his army; despite this he defeated the enemy almost single-handedly. Reports of his victory are written on most of the temples that he built:

> *"He mounted his horse and started out alone. All his ground was ablaze with fire. His eyes were savage as he beheld the enemy. He slaughtered them in their places, they sprawled before his horse, and His Majesty was alone."*

Far left: A painted carving of a royal couple from the time of Akhenaten. The queen is offering the king a flower

Left: A portrait of Tutankhamun as the god Nefertum who was born from a lotus flower

Right: Ramesses attacking his enemies from a chariot

THE 3RD INTERMEDIATE AND LATE PERIODS (Dynasties 21-30)

During this time Egypt was once again divided into small areas ruled by different dynasties at the same time, each of which had its own capital city. The priests and pristesses of the god Amun became very powerful at this time. The high priest and high prietess ruled in Luxor, while other dynasties ruled in Lower Egypt. During this time Egypt was invaded and ruled by many foreigners, including Libyans, Nubians, Assyrians and Persians.

THE GRAECO-ROMAN PERIOD

When Alexander the Great, a Macedonian prince, defeated the Persians who were ruling Egypt he became pharaoh in 332 BC. He founded the town of Alexandria and named it after himself. He is believed to be buried there although his tomb has never been found. After Alexander died one of his generals, called Ptolemy, ruled Egypt and founded the last Egyptian dynasty: the Ptolemaic dynasty.

The Ptolemies' capital was at Alexandria, on the Mediterranean coast. The family was a mixture of Greek and Egyptian: they spoke Greek and Egyptian, could probably also read hieroglyphs, and had Greek and Egyptian gods.

Below: A tomb from Alexandria, showing the dead person being mummified. The gods are wearing a mixture of Egyptian and Greek clothes

The most famous of the Ptolemies was Queen Cleopatra VII, the last of the family and the last pharaoh of Egypt.

Cleopatra wanted to remain friendly with the Romans who were very powerful, but she also wanted to protect Egypt from being invaded by them. She allied herself first with Julius Caesar, and later with Mark Antony, another Roman general. However, Mark Antony quarreled with the Roman ruler Augustus. They fought a battle which Mark Antony and Cleopatra lost.

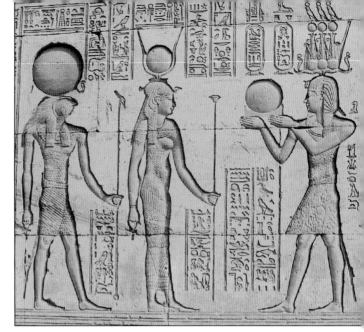

Above: This is the only known ancient Egyptian picture of Cleopatra VII (in the centre). Ancient writers say that she was a strong ruler with a powerful personality

Cleopatra did not want to be taken prisoner by Augustus so, according to Roman historians, she allowed a poisonous snake to bite her. After her death Egypt became a part of the Roman Empire and was not ruled by an Egyptian again for over 1,500 years.

Time line of the Kingdoms

c3050 BC Foundation of the Egyptian state

2920–2575 BC Early Dynastic Period

2575–2134 BC OLD KINGDOM

2134–2040 BC 1st Intermediate Period

2040–1640 BC MIDDLE KINGDOM

1640–1532 BC 2nd Intermediate Period

Some important pharaohs

OLD KINGDOM
1st Dynasty
Menes (=Narmer)

2nd Dynasty
Hetepsekhemny
Peribsen

3rd Dynasty
Djoser
Sekhemket
Huni

4th Dynasty
Snefru
Khufu (=Cheops)
Khafre
  (=Chephren)
Menkaure
Shepseskaf

5th Dynasty
Userkaf
Sahure
Neferefre
Neuserre
Unas

6th Dynasty
Teti

Pepi I
Merenre
Pepi II

MIDDLE
KINGDOM
11th Dynasty
Mentuhotep II

12th Dynasty
Amenemhat I
Senusert I
Amenemhat II
Senusert II
Senusert III
Amenemhat III
Amenemhat IV

NEW KINGDOM
18th Dynasty
Ahmose I
Amenhotep I
Tuthmosis I
Tuthmosis II
Hatshepsut
Tuthmosis III
Amenhotep II
Tuthmosis IV

Amenhotep III
Akhenaten
Tutankhamun
Horemheb

19th Dynasty
Ramesses I
Seti I
Ramesses II
Merneptah

20th Dynasty
Ramesses III
Ramesses IV
Ramesses XI

THIRD
INTERMEDIATE
PERIOD
21st Dynasty
Psusennes I
Osorkon I

22nd Dynasty
Sheshonq I
Osorkon II

25th Dynasty
Piye
Shabaka

Taharqa

LATE PERIOD
26th Dynasty
Psamtik I
Psamtik II
Apries
Amasis II
Psamtik III

30th Dynasty
Nectanebo I
Nectanebo II

Alexander the
Great

GRAECO-
ROMAN PERIOD
Ptolemy I
Ptolemy II
Ptolemy V
Cleopatra VII

NEW KINGDOM

1070–712 BC
3rd Intermediate Period

712–332 BC
Late Period

332 BC–AD 395
Graeco-Roman Period

Glossary

Dynasty	A division of Egyptian history, made up of several kings who ruled one after the other
Hyksos	A word that comes from the ancient Egyptian, meaning "Rulers of the Foreign Lands"
Kingdom	A division of Egyptian history. There are three kingdoms in Egyptian history: the Old, the Middle and the New. These were the times when Egypt was united and ruled by one king.
Lower Egypt	The north of the country, from roughly just south of Cairo up to the Mediterranean
Pharaoh	The god-king of Egypt
Upper Egypt	The south of the country, from just south of Cairo as far as Aswan

---

Photo credits

copyright and photography by Salima Ikram: p3 (relief from temple of Seti I, Abydos); p5 (relief from Kalabsha); p8 (relief from Giza); p11 (relief from Abydos); p22 (skull, Egyptian Museum); p24 (painting from Deir El Bahari); p23 top (both paintings Egyptian Museum); p26 left (carving, Berlin Museum); p27 (relief from Thebes); p29 (relief from Dendera)

copyright Hoopoe Books: p4 by Ayman El Kharrat (palette, Egyptian Museum); p7 by Tim Loveless (relief from statue, Luxor); p14 by Tim Loveless; p15 by Ayman El Kharrat (palette, Egyptian Museum); pp18-19 by Ayman El Kharrat (models, Egyptian Museum); pp20-21 by Ayman El Kharrat (statue, Egyptian Museum); p25 bottom by Tim Loveless (obelisk, Karnak Temple); p26 right by Ayman El Kharrat (statue, Egyptian Museum); p28 by Tim Loveless (tomb in Anfushi, Alexandria)

Index